Raintree is an imprint of Capstone Global Library Limited,
a company incorporated in England and Wales having its
registered office at 7 Pilgrim Street, London, EC4V 6LB –
Registered company number: 6695582

www.raintreepublishers.co.uk
myorders@raintreepublishers.co.uk

First published by Stone Arch Books © 2013
First published in the United Kingdom in 2014
The moral rights of the proprietor have been asserted

Originally published by DC Comics in
the U.S. in single magazine form as
Batman: The Brave and the Bold #6.
Copyright © 2013 DC Comics. All Rights Reserved.

Ashley C. Andersen Zantop Publisher
Michael Dahl Editorial Director
Donald Lemke & Sean Tulien Editors
Heather Kindseth Creative Director
Hilary Wacholz Designer
Kathy McColley Production Specialist

DC COMICS
Rachel Gluckstern & Michael Siglain Original U.S. Editors
Harvey Richards U.S. Assistant Editor

ISBN 978 1 406 26650 4
17 16 15 14 13
10 9 8 7 6 5 4 3 2 1

Printed and bound in China by Leo Paper Products Ltd

British Library Cataloguing in Publication Data
A full catalogue record for this book is available from the British Library

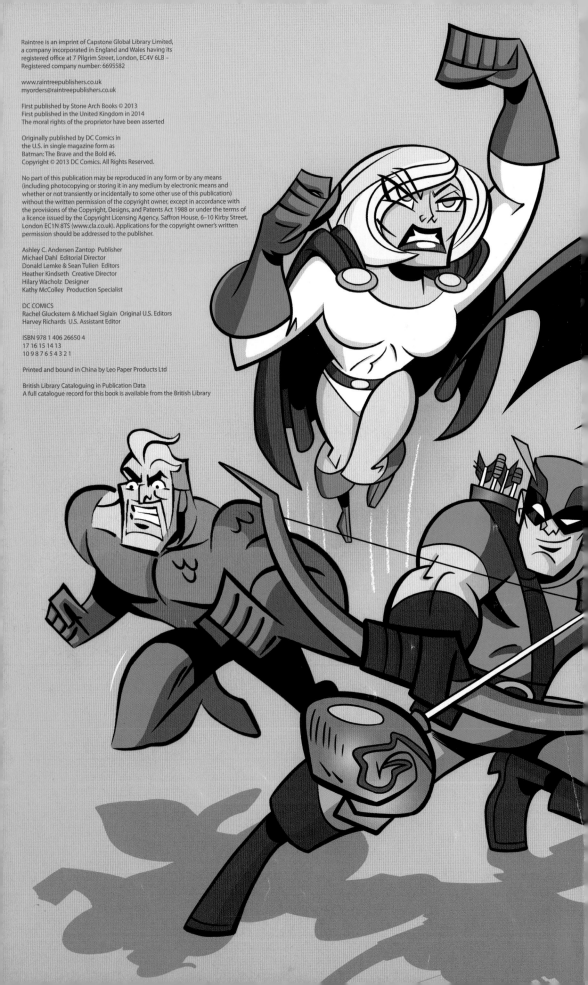

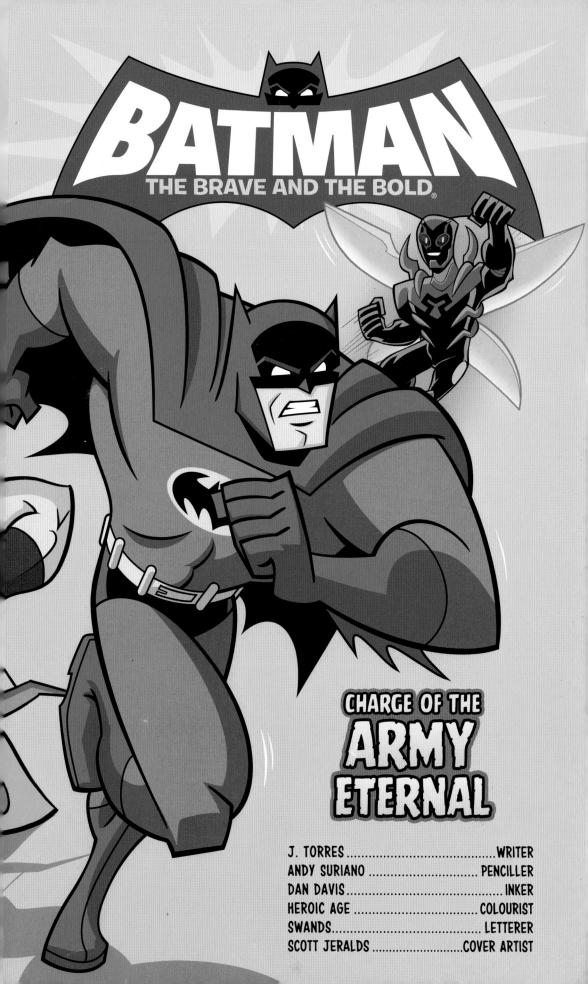

BATMAN
THE BRAVE AND THE BOLD.

CHARGE OF THE
ARMY
ETERNAL

J. TORRES ....WRITER
ANDY SURIANO .... PENCILLER
DAN DAVIS..INKER
HEROIC AGE ....COLOURIST
SWANDS...LETTERER
SCOTT JERALDS ....COVER ARTIST

RRRAH!

...AND I DON'T SPAR WITH 5TH CENTURY GREEK WARRIORS EVERY DAY EITHER!

THIS...

...IS...

...NOT...

...SPARTAAA!

WHAM

SPARTANS HERE TODAY... THE TIME MACHINE THAT WENT MISSING FROM S.T.A.R. LABS YESTERDAY...

BUT THREE MEN ISN'T MUCH OF AN ARMY FOR YOU TO COMMAND. SLOWING DOWN IN YOUR *OLD* AGE?

I THOUGHT I COULD BETTER HANDLE *THREE* SOLDIERS...

...WHEN THE *FOUR* OUTLAWS I TRANSPORTED FROM THE OLD WEST WOULDN'T TAKE ORDERS...

...LET ME GUESS, *GENERAL IMMORTUS.* THIS IS PART OF SOME HAREBRAINED SCHEME TO RECRUIT SOLDIERS FROM THE *PAST* FOR YOUR WARPED WAR GAMES AGAINST GOOD PEOPLE, LIKE THE MEMBERS OF THE DOOM PATROL!

...AND I ONLY BROUGHT THEM HERE AFTER THE *SIX* FROM THE ORDER OF THE BLACK KNIGHT, ER, DESERTED ME...

...WHICH HAPPENED SHORTLY AFTER I LOST, UH, CONTROL OF THE *TWELVE* OR SO VIKING RAIDERS!

KA-KLUNK

YOU CAN *THANK* ME LATER FOR SAVING YOUR LIFE *AND* CLEANING UP YOUR MESS.

I CALLED YOU TO *RESCUE* ME! NOT LOCK ME UP! YOU CAN'T KEEP THE "FOREVER SOLDIER" HERE FOREVER, YOU KNOW!

STAY RIGHT HERE WHILE I DO SOME RECRUITING MYSELF.

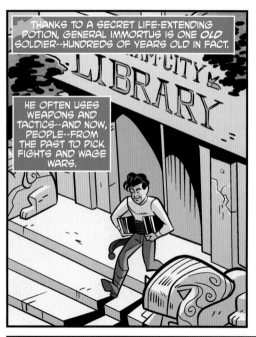

THANKS TO A SECRET LIFE-EXTENDING POTION, GENERAL IMMORTUS IS ONE *OLD* SOLDIER--HUNDREDS OF YEARS OLD IN FACT.

HE OFTEN USES WEAPONS AND TACTICS--AND NOW, PEOPLE--FROM THE PAST TO PICK FIGHTS AND WAGE WARS.

I NEEDED HELP FIGHTING FIRE WITH FIRE AND I KNEW JUST THE RIGHT "MATCH" FOR THIS TASK.

BATMAN! WHAT... WHAT ARE YOU DOING HERE?

ERRRT!

KID ETERNITY! YOU HAVE THE ABILITY TO SUMMON HISTORICAL AND MYTHICAL *HEROES* OF OLD AND USE THEIR POWERS TO FIGHT EVIL IN THE PRESENT!

I NEED YOUR HELP ROUNDING UP OUTLAWS AND VILLAINS FROM THE PAST WHO ARE RUNNING AMOK IN OUR TIME!

OH BOY! IT ISN'T EVERY DAY THAT I GET A CALL FOR HELP FROM BATMAN!

VRRROOOM

11

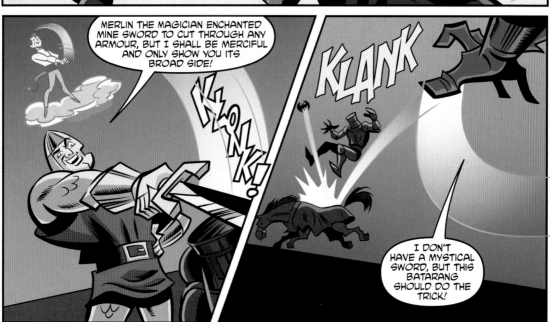

"ANOTHER GOOD CALL, KID! THE VIKING PRINCE WAS A SCANDINAVIAN ROYAL AND LEGENDARY SWORDSMAN..."

...WHO WAS MADE INVULNERABLE TO MAN-MADE WEAPONS BY THE NORSE GOD ODIN, SO HE REALLY CAN'T BE HARMED BY ANY OF THESE GUYS!

MAYBE I SHOULD SIT THIS ONE OUT AND JUST WAIT FOR HIM TO BRING THEM ALL DOWN?

YEAH, RIGHT! IT'S NOT EVERY DAY THAT I GET TO FIGHT VIKINGS!

SO, WHAT ARE YOU DOING HERE WITH THAT TIME MACHINE? HAVEN'T YOU LEARNED--

FROM MY PAST MISTAKES? OH, YES. "HE WHO DOES NOT LEARN FROM HISTORY..."

"...IS DOOMED TO REPEAT IT!"

PRECISELY, BOY. AND THAT'S WHY I SEARCHED THE AGES FOR AN ARTIFACT, A *WEAPON*, WHICH WOULD GIVE ME THE POWER TO COMMAND ANY SOLDIER, ANY ARMY THAT I DESIRE!

THIS IS THE *SPEAR OF DESTINY!*

HE WHO WIELDS IT CAN COMMAND *ANY* ARMY TO DO *ANYTHING* HE WANTS! AND AN ARMY LED BY HE WHO POSSESSES THE SPEAR...

"...CANNOT BE DEFEATED BY *ANY* MAN BORN OF A WOMAN"!

YES, A ROBOT! BUT NOT JUST ANY ROBOT, BUT A SOLDIER *MANUFACTURED* AND *PROGRAMMED*, NOT "BORN," FOR WAR!

JUDGING FROM YOUR REACTION, IMMORTUS, I GAVE THE KID THE RIGHT ORDER!

IT'S ONLY A MATTER OF TIME BEFORE G.I. ROBOT DEFEATS YOUR EVIL ARMY, SO WHY DON'T YOU MAKE IT EASIER ON YOURSELF AND SURRENDER NOW?

ALL RIGHT, ALL RIGHT... I'M GETTING TOO OLD FOR THIS!

LATER...

THAT'S IT! THE SPARTANS ARE BACK IN ANCIENT GREECE, THE KNIGHTS ARE BACK IN MEDIEVAL TIMES, AND EVERYONE ELSE IS BACK WHERE THEY BELONG!

WHAT ABOUT GENERAL IMMORTUS?

I'LL TAKE HIM TO IRON HEIGHTS PRISON BEFORE I RETURN THIS TIME MACHINE TO S.T.A.R. LABS.

GEE, I'VE READ THAT IRON HEIGHTS CAN BE A PRETTY TOUGH PLACE! I KIND OF FEEL SORRY FOR THE OLD MAN. ISN'T THERE SOMEWHERE ELSE HE CAN GO?

LIKE WHERE?

OH, I DON'T KNOW... MAYBE... THE GOLDEN AGE RETIREMENT HOME?

HA-HA-HA-HA!

KIDS THESE DAYS! NO RESPECT FOR THEIR ELDERS!

End

GENERAL IMMORTUS

General Immortus has lived for centuries due to a secret "life-extending potion". He has spent his very long life fighting on the wrong side of various wars, including the war on crime.

TOP SECRET:
Also known as the "Forever Soldier", General Immortus seems forever doomed to repeat the mistakes of his past crimes, time and time again.

KID ETERNITY

ANDY
DAN D.

By uttering the magic word "Eternity!" Kid Eternity can summon any historical, legendary, or even mythological hero, and use their powers to battle the forces of evil. Not much else is known about "The Kid", but some speculate he is related to Captain Marvel and the Marvel Family, while others believe he is connected to the Lords of Order and Chaos.

CREATORS

J. TORRES WRITER

J. Torres won the Shuster Award for Outstanding Writer for his work on *Batman: Legends of the Dark Knight*, *Love As a Foreign Language*, and *Teen Titans Go*. He is also the writer of the Eisner Award nominated *Alison Dare* and the YALSA listed *Days Like This* and *Lola: A Ghost Story*. Other comic book credits include *Avatar: The Last Airbender*, *Legion of Super-Heroes in the 31st Century*, *Ninja Scroll*, *Wonder Girl*, *Wonder Woman*, and *WALL·E: Recharge*.

ANDY SURIANO PENCILLER

Andy Suriano is an illustrator of both comic books and animation. His comic book credits include *Batman: The Brave and the Bold* and *Doc Bizarre, M.D.* He's worked on popular animated television series as well, such as *Samurai Jack* and *Star Wars: The Clone Wars*.

DAN DAVIS INKER

Dan Davis is a comic illustrator for DC Comics, Warner Bros., and Bongo. His work has been nominated for several Eisner Awards, including his work on *Batman: The Brave and the Bold*. During his career, Davis has illustrated Batman, The Simpsons, Harry Potter, Samurai Jack, and many other well-known characters!

GLOSSARY

amok wild frenzy

artefact object made in the past

distress feeling of great pain or sadness

harebrained foolish or absurd

insubordinate not submitting to authority; rebellious

medieval to do with the Middle Ages, the period of history between AD 500 and 1450.

merciful compassionate, lenient, or forgiving

spar strike or fight with another

VISUAL QUESTIONS & PROMPTS

1 Based on what you know about Kid Eternity from this comic book, what do you think he was studying at the library? Use specific panels to support your opinion.

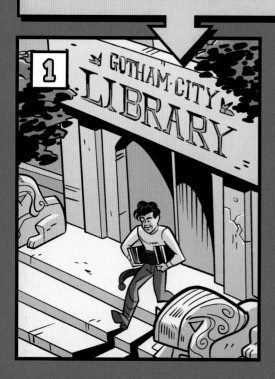

2 Based on what you know about General Immortus from this comic book, what probably happened in the panel at right? Why are the Spartans there? Why are they attacking the General?

3. Why do you think Batman is coloured solid black in this panel? How does Batman's appearance make you feel?

4. Why do you think the borders of this panel are jagged? What effect does it create?

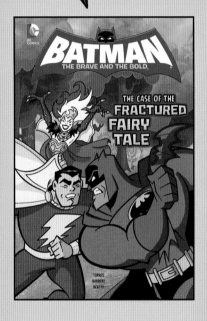

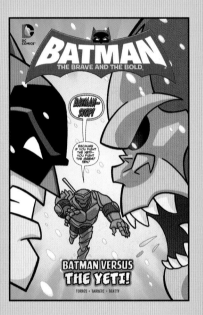

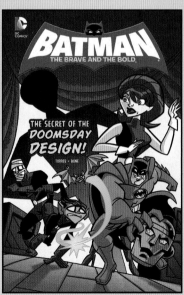